CCSS **Genre** Expository Text

Essential Question

How does technology lead to discoveries?

LOOKING FURTHER

THE HUBBLE TELESCOPE

BY BILL NAGELKERKE

INTRODUCTION

The two parts of the word *telescope* come from the Greek language. *Tele* means "a long way," and scope means "to see." A telescope helps people see things that are far away.

Before telescopes were invented, an ancient Greek named Aristarchus suggested that Earth orbited around the sun. He was probably the first person to suggest this idea. Because there were no telescopes, he was not able to **verify** his **deduction**. However, he was sure it was right.

By 1609, the Italian scientist Galileo had made a refracting telescope. Refracting telescopes bend light through a glass lens. This makes faraway objects look larger. Galileo used the telescope to study the sky. One of Galileo's telescopes could make objects appear up to 20 times larger.

Galileo used his telescope to discover sunspots and Jupiter's moons.

(t) NASA, ESA, S. Beckwith (STScI) and the HUDF Team, (b) National Geographic Society/Corbis

Several decades later, the English astronomer Isaac Newton made a reflecting telescope. A reflecting telescope uses mirrors instead of lenses to **capture**, or catch, light rays.

The Hubble Space Telescope is a type of reflecting telescope. Hubble has let astronomers observe deep into space and discover **galaxies**.

Today, astronomers do not peer through telescopes. They view images recorded by electronic **devices** in the telescopes. The Hubble telescope operates by using these electronic machines.

The United States and Europe worked together to create the Hubble telescope.

CHAPTER 1

LAND OR SKY?

Telescopes enabled people to learn new information. For example, Galileo gazed at the moon through his telescope, and he saw that it has craters. Before this, people thought the moon was smooth.

People began to produce telescopes that were bigger and better. In 1873, a company created the largest telescope in the world. Scientists used this telescope to discover that Mars has two moons.

The Lick **Observatory** in California was built in 1887. Although it was the first permanent mountaintop observatory, it continues to operate. In 1897, the Yerkes Observatory in Wisconsin opened. Yerkes still has the world's largest refracting telescope.

Through his telescope, Galileo was able to see the craters on the moon.

Then a German rocket scientist named Hermann Oberth had an idea. He proposed flying a telescope into space by rocket. He thought this would enable us to observe even farther than we could by using the **optical** telescopes on Earth.

Four satellites carrying telescopes were sent into space between 1966 and 1972. They were called Optical Astronomical Observatories (OAOs).

Optical and Radio Telescopes

Optical and radio telescopes are two types of telescopes. Optical telescopes capture the light we can see with our eyes. Hubble is an optical telescope.

Radio telescopes use radio waves to create images. We can't see radio waves, but stars and galaxies send them out.

NASA

Astronomers learned a lot from these early orbiting telescopes. This knowledge **ultimately** helped them build even better telescopes. In 1990, a space shuttle carried the Hubble Space Telescope into orbit. The Hubble was named after an important American astronomer, Edwin Hubble.

Hubble now orbits 353 miles (568 kilometers) above Earth. The pictures it takes are some of the clearest ever seen of **celestial** objects.

The Hubble Space Telescope

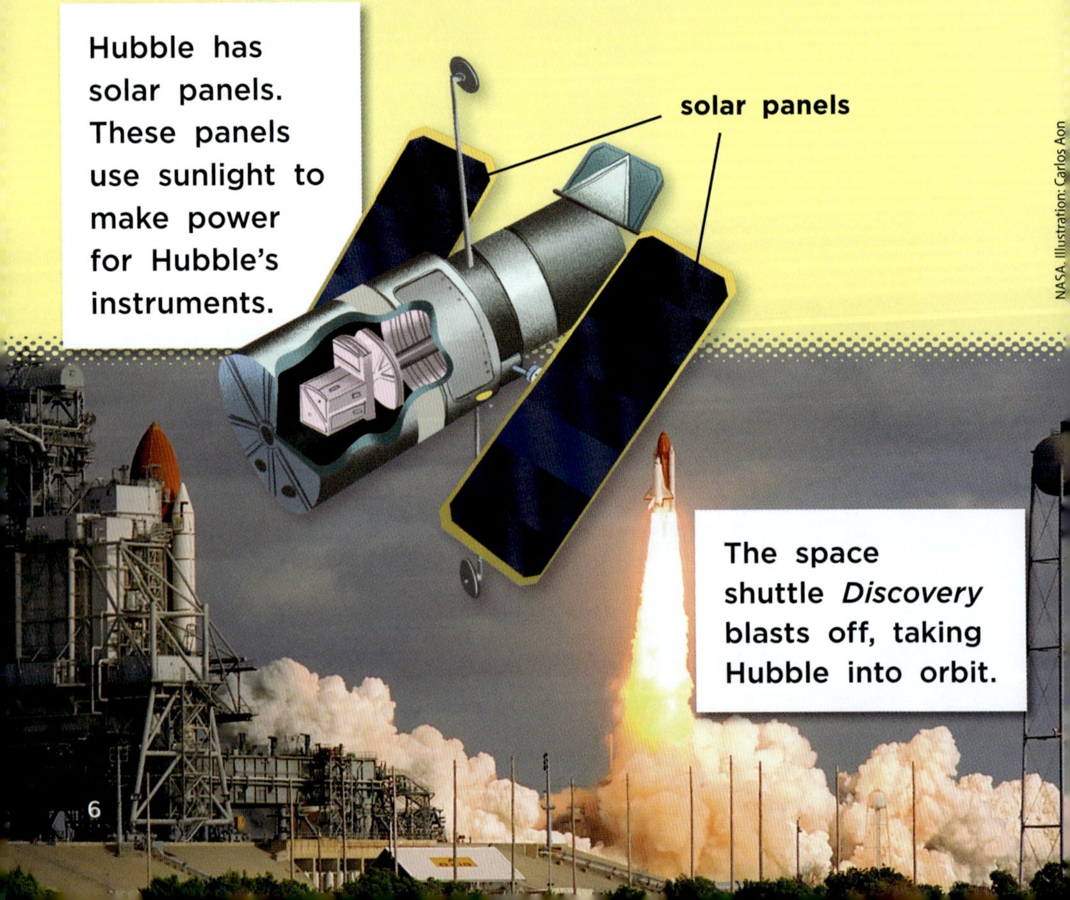

NASA. Illustration: Carlos Aon

When Hubble was first **launched**, events did not go well. After Hubble was lifted into orbit, scientists found problems with its main mirror and solar panels.

In 1993, **NASA** sent astronauts to repair the problems on Hubble. The astronauts traveled to Hubble by space shuttle. The mission was a success.

Astronauts used the space shuttle's robotic arm to fix Hubble.

From high above Earth's **atmosphere**, Hubble collected **massive** amounts of information. Hubble sent this huge volume of data back to Earth.

STOP AND CHECK

Why is it helpful to have a telescope in space?

Edwin Hubble

Edwin Hubble worked at an observatory in California in the 1920s. He studied spiral nebulae, which are clouds of dust and gas in space. He also proved that the universe is expanding.

CHAPTER 2

THE AMAZING HUBBLE

Light takes time to travel. Some galaxies are vast distances away, so their light can take billions of years to reach us. Scientists believe Hubble's pictures show us how parts of space looked billions of years ago. The light has taken all that time to reach Hubble.

At one point, Hubble observed an area of space that appeared empty. Scientists were amazed when Hubble sent pictures back to Earth. They were surprised because the images showed thousands of new galaxies. This part of space is now known as the Hubble Deep Field.

Scientists have used Hubble's information to **estimate**, or figure out, the age of the universe. Hubble's data helped astronomers discover that the universe is expanding, or moving apart, faster. It is not slowing down as some had thought.

Hubble's amazing images show the beauty of space.

NASA scientists in Greenbelt, Maryland, control Hubble. They use satellites to send radio messages to Hubble, and the telescope sends information back to Earth in the same way.

Hubble's information is then sent to the Space Telescope Science Institute in Baltimore, Maryland. NASA scientists' **colleagues** around the world can use the information in their own research.

Capturing Data from the Stars

This diagram shows how Hubble sends data to the Space Telescope Science Institute.

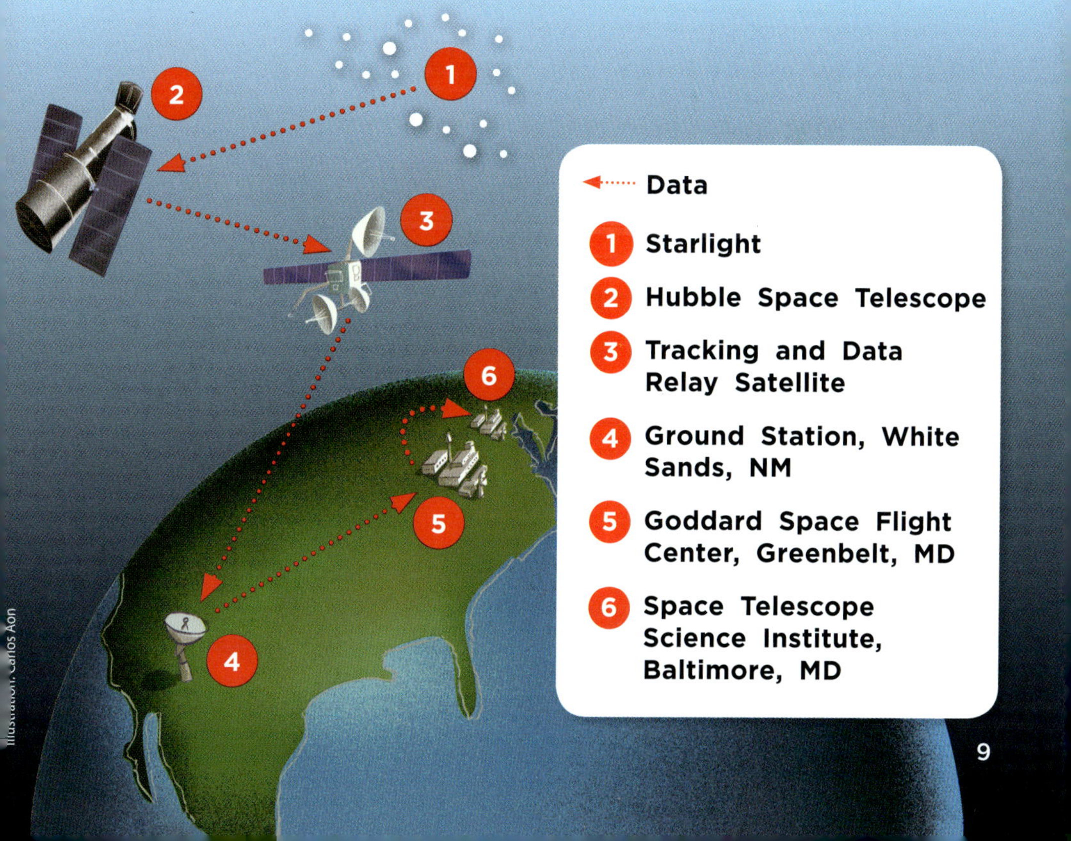

Young scientists study Hubble's information, too. College students work with the Space Telescope Science Institute to examine Hubble data. They also hear experts talk about astronomy.

The Institute has established the Hubble Deep Field Academy Web site. On this Web site, younger students can study the pictures of galaxies from the Hubble Deep Field.

Ariel Skelley/Blend Images/Getty Images

Students also study the Web site to learn how astronomers use Hubble's data.

This is the clearest Deep Field picture yet.

The academy students learn about the huge distances between objects in space. They also find out how astronomers use light-years to measure those distances. A light-year is the distance that light can travel in a year. This is about 6 trillion (6,000,000,000,000) miles.

One object in the Deep Field is 12 billion light-years away from Earth. It takes light from this galaxy 12 billion years to reach Earth.

NASA, ESA, S. Beckwith (STScI) and the HUDF Team

STOP AND CHECK

What has Hubble shown astronomers?

CHAPTER 3

HUBBLE'S LAST DAYS

In 1997, astronauts **installed** a special camera on Hubble. The camera that they put in place takes images of **infrared light**. This light comes from faraway galaxies. Hubble's older cameras could not see that far. The astronauts also installed a new **spectrograph** to help Hubble look for **black holes**.

In 1999, astronauts replaced special wheels, called gyroscopes, on Hubble. These wheels are devices that let scientists on Earth point Hubble in different directions.

(t) NASA, ESA, S. Beckwith (STScI) and the HUDF Team, (b) NASA

When astronauts repair Hubble, they attach it to the space shuttle.

In 2002, another type of camera was installed on Hubble. This one was more powerful and a lot faster than Hubble's other cameras. The astronauts also updated Hubble's solar panels.

In 2009, another space shuttle visited Hubble. On this trip, astronauts updated some of Hubble's equipment. This will help it stay in orbit longer. Since the space shuttle program is now finished, no other shuttles will visit Hubble in the future.

Deep Field and Ultra Deep Field

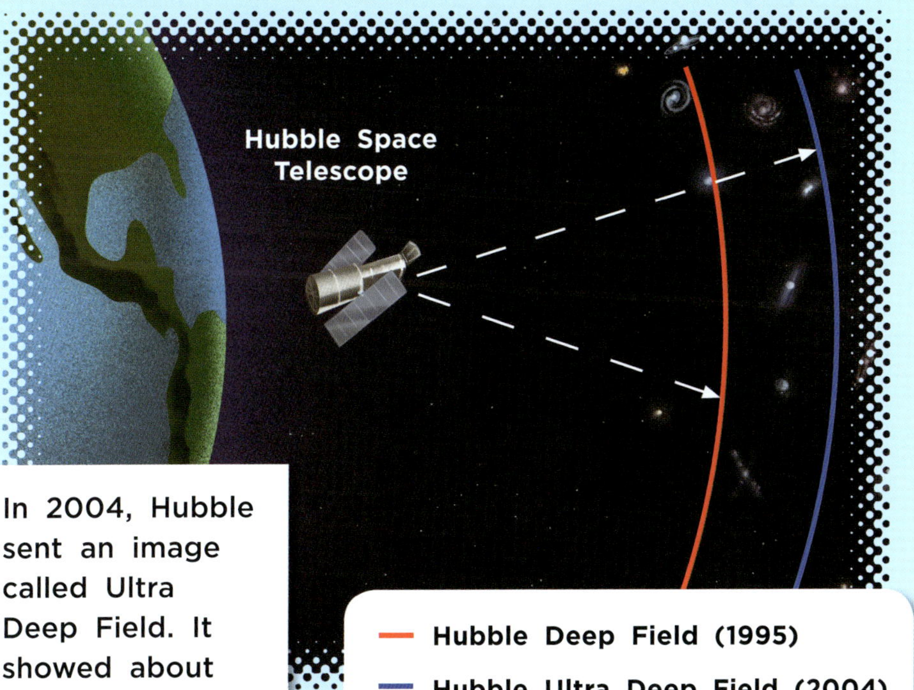

In 2004, Hubble sent an image called Ultra Deep Field. It showed about 10,000 galaxies.

Illustration: Carlos Aon

Hubble made its one-millionth observation on July 4, 2011. This drawing shows an artist's idea of the planet and star that Hubble observed.

Hubble will probably stay in orbit for a few more years. If it lasts until 2020, it will have been in orbit for 30 years. This is **impressive** and exciting because its life in space was **conservatively** estimated to be only 15 years!

One day, Hubble's parts will stop working and it will be guided back to Earth. Although Hubble will no longer orbit Earth, this does not mean the end of telescopes in space.

NASA, ESA, and G. Bacon (STScI)

Hubble Facts

- Hubble weighs 27,000 pounds. This is the same as two full-grown elephants.
- Hubble travels around Earth once every 97 minutes, moving at about 5 miles per second.
- Hubble can see ten times more clearly than the best telescopes on Earth.
- If you could see as well as Hubble can, you could stand in New York City and see two fireflies in San Francisco.

(bkgd) NASA, ESA, S. Beckwith (STScI) and the HUDF Team

In 2003, NASA launched the Spitzer Space Telescope. This telescope has detected planets outside our solar system. It has also discovered that Saturn has an extra ring.

There are plans for further exploration by orbiting telescopes. One is the James Webb Space Telescope.

The Webb telescope will carry equipment that can measure different types of light. A huge shield will protect the telescope from the sun. The Webb telescope's main job will be to study the history of the universe.

STOP AND CHECK

Why will the Hubble stop working?

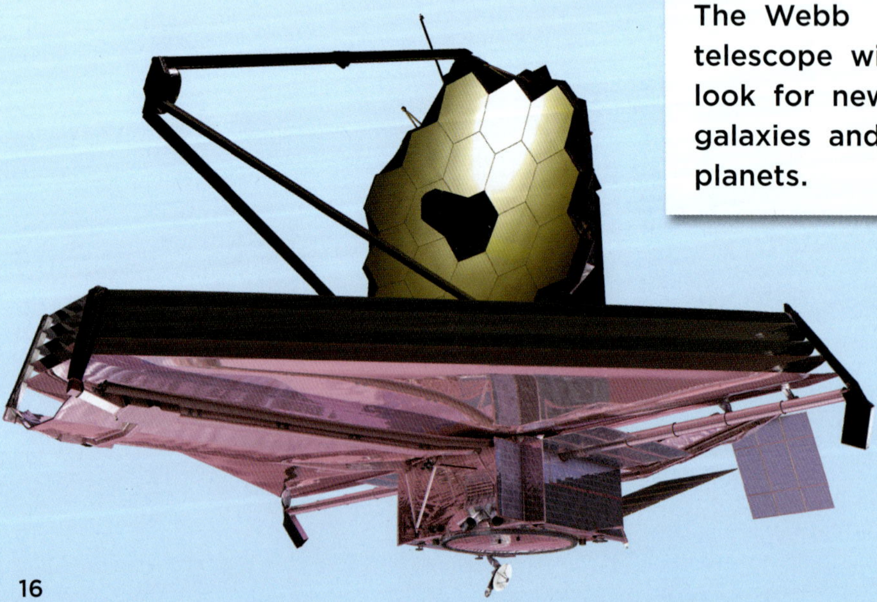

The Webb telescope will look for new galaxies and planets.

NASA

CONCLUSION

The Hubble Space Telescope is one of NASA's most successful and longest-lasting missions. Now scientists are planning a new **era**, or period of time, in space telescopes. The Webb telescope will have a mirror that is seven times bigger than Hubble's mirror.

Scientists will also keep studying the sky using radio telescopes on Earth. One of these is the Square Kilometre Array. This telescope is so complex that we cannot understand its data yet.

These changes mean that there is an abundance of work ahead for astronomers. There are many more exciting discoveries to be made.

(b) Jonathan Larsen/iStock/Getty Images Plus/Getty Images, (t) NASA, ESA, S. Beckwith (STScI) and the HUDF Team

The Square Kilometre Array will have 3,000 radio telescopes.

Respond to Reading

Summarize

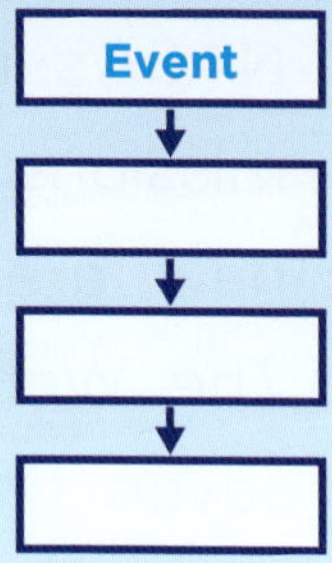

Use details from the text to summarize *Looking Further*. Your graphic organizer may help you.

Text Evidence

1. What steps led to people building space-based telescopes? **SEQUENCE**

2. Find the term *spiral nebulae* on page 7. What clues can you find to help you figure out the meaning? **VOCABULARY**

3. Write about how the telescope changed from Galileo's time to today. Use events from the text to help you. **WRITE ABOUT READING**

CCSS **Genre** Science Fiction

Compare Texts

Read a story about how scientists used telescopes to make an unusual discovery.

The Watchers

The spaceship began orbiting the planet. The crew had named the planet Elektron.

In the control room, everyone was feeling nervous. Finally, they were close to another planet that could **sustain** human life.

All eyes were fixed on the SK-ope. The crew was excited because the views through the SK-ope showed the planet up close.

"There are oceans, forests, and clean air."

"It looks just like Old Earth!"

Illustration: Carlos Aon

"The telescopes weren't wrong—they've found us the perfect home."

The crew turned away from the SK-ope, all talking at once. But Commander Diaz stayed by the SK-ope, her lips pulled tight.

"The data from the telescopes are so strong," Diaz thought. They had been searching for years, and the evidence was too good to ignore.

And yet...Diaz had the feeling that something was wrong. She looked more closely at the screen. Suddenly she shivered, and the hairs on the back of her neck stood up.

"Shall we land, Commander?" asked Second Officer Nowak.

Commander Diaz paused, then nodded. She had no reason not to give the order. She just had an odd feeling.

"Everyone prepare for descent," Nowak said. The engine **droned** as the ship slowed down.

Diaz stayed near the SK-ope.

"Commander? You should get ready," Nowak said.

But Diaz couldn't move away from the screen.

"Can we turn around?" Diaz asked.

"No, it's too late," Nowak said. "What did you see, Commander Diaz?"

"I saw people," the Commander murmured. "They had a telescope and they were looking at me."

"Who . . . what . . . are they?" Nowak asked.

"They're Watchers. That's what they were doing. They were watching me watching them. They were waiting."

She turned the SK-ope to its lowest level. She wanted to stop her crew from seeing the pictures.

They were pictures of faces, familiar faces. One was the Commander's own face, looking back at her. The Watchers looked just like them.

Make Connections

How did the scientists use technology to discover the planet Elektron? **ESSENTIAL QUESTION**

How do *Looking Further* and *The Watchers* show the importance of telescopes in exploring the universe? **TEXT TO TEXT**

Illustration: Carlos Aon

Glossary

atmosphere *(AT-muhs-feer)* the gases that surround planets, including Earth ***(page 7)***

black holes *(blak HOHLS)* parts of space with such strong gravity that not even light can escape, making them appear black and empty ***(page 12)***

celestial *(suh-LES-chuhl)* relating to the sky ***(page 6)***

infrared light *(in-fruh-RED light)* a type of light that cannot be seen but is given off by objects above a certain temperature ***(page 12)***

NASA *(NA-suh)* National Aeronautics and Space Administration, the U.S. space exploration agency ***(page 7)***

observatory *(uhb-ZUHR-vuh-tor-ee)* a place with equipment to study the sky ***(page 4)***

optical *(OP-ti-kuhl)* seen with the eye ***(page 5)***

spectrograph *(SPEK-truh-graf)* a device that can split light into its different colors and photograph them ***(page 12)***

Index

Focus on Science

Purpose To understand the differences between telescopes on Earth and telescopes in space

Procedure You will need poster paper or board, glue, and markers.

Step 1 With a partner, reread *Looking Further.* Write down two or three facts about telescopes on Earth and telescopes in space.

Step 2 Use an educational Internet site to find pictures or diagrams of the two types of telescopes.

Step 3 Make a poster showing each type of telescope. Under the diagram or picture, write the facts you have found.

Step 4 Present your poster to the class.

Conclusion What did you discover about the two types of telescopes?